48 Self Esteem Activities for Women

*Powerful Exercises for
Overcoming Low Self Esteem
Plus 50 Positive Affirmations on
How to Love Yourself!*

Corinna Bowers

Table of Contents

Introduction

As a life coach, I work with a lot of women who find themselves struggling with the pain, isolation, and negativity that often stem from low self esteem.

Because no matter if self esteem issues have been prevalent for you your entire life or if your self esteem is generally high with occasional low bouts, when you're in the depths of struggling with negative feelings about yourself, your relationships, and your future, you know how hard it is to feel strong, content, and valuable.

If any of this sounds familiar to you, you've found this book at just the right time!

Low self esteem can be a difficult burden to bear, especially if it is a roadblock to your happiness and success.

The great news though is that you have a lot of control over how you see and feel about yourself. Sometimes all you need is direction, encouragement, and a sense of progress and you too can begin to enjoy the confidence and satisfaction that comes with higher self esteem.

I designed these effective self esteem activities based on what's worked for me personally, and what's worked for my coaching clients. I'm confident they'll work for you too.

Sending many good wishes your way!

Corinna Bowers
Life Coach
www.focused-momentum-lifecoach.com

How to Use This Book

Always be a first-rate version of yourself,
instead of a second-rate version of somebody else.
~ Judy Garland

This book presents and explains a variety of dynamic self esteem activities organized under the three main self- improvement categories that most impact your level of happiness and sense of self.

These three categories are: **Developing Your Essence**, **Improving Your Connections**, and **Controlling Your Destiny**.

The first category, **Developing Your Essence**, contains activities that focus on strengthening your beliefs about yourself as a worthy human being. Feeling valuable, confident, determined, capable, good enough, and able to improve are essential beliefs for living with a sense of comfort, peace, and optimism.

The second category, **Improving Your Connections**, contains activities that focus on increasing your connection with yourself, others, and your community. Feeling bonded to people and places is an important way to stay grounded in reality, feel supported and loved, and feel a part of the bigger picture.

The third category, **Controlling Your Destiny**, contains activities that focus on reclaiming your power and taking the direction of your life into your own hands. Refusing to feel like a victim and instead making choices that enhance your well being and sense of self makes you feel strong and sure-footed, even during uncertain times.

If you doubt you can accomplish something,
then you can't accomplish it.
You have to have confidence in your ability,
and then be tough enough to follow through.
~Rosalyn Smith Carter

Each of these exercises can be effective on its own or as a perfect complement to your current self improvement efforts.

Depending on your particular needs, you can try a new activity each day or spend an entire week focusing on a particular exercise. You may choose to skip through this book, picking and choosing self esteem exercises as they strike you, or you may systematically go through each activity page by page.

You may find that some of these exercises seem similar to each other. While there may be similarities, in fact each activity has a different and specific focus and provides unique benefits. Any apparent overlap can be used as an opportunity to strengthen particular characteristics.

Each activity contains a *To Do* section with suggested actions to complete the exercise. You may find that the suggestions plant a new thought that sends you in a new and positive direction. Other times you may find that the suggested actions provide helpful ideas and structure. The *To Do* suggestions are just a basic framework for how to follow through on each exercise but they are only offered as options, not directives.

Remember that self improvement strategies aren't one size fits all. Anyone looking to build her self esteem will enjoy and benefit from these exercises, but you may find that not every exercise resonates with you right now, and that's okay!

Take what you can from the exercises you connect with now and revisit the others at another point in the future. Remember, no matter how cheesy this sounds, personal development is a life-long journey, not a specific destination. So the methods you set aside today may be a better fit for you down the road.

You have within you right now, everything you need to deal with whatever the world can throw at you.
~Brian Tracy

This book is to be used for entertainment purposes only. It is not a substitute for professional help which should be sought if needed. Caution must always be used when interacting with others on the internet.

<u>Developing Your Essence</u>

The most important opinion you have
is the one you have of yourself,
and the most significant things you say all day
are those things you say to yourself.
~ Unknown Author

This section focuses on strengthening your beliefs about yourself as a valuable human being. This is a key component to good self esteem and, for many women, needs to be continually assessed and confirmed.

Feeling worthy, confident, determined, capable, good enough, and able to improve are essential for a life filled with a sense of comfort, peace, and optimism.

The activities in this section work directly on negative attitudes, feelings of inadequacy, and perceived limitations.

Self Esteem Activity #1
Use Affirmations

Affirmations are one of the easiest ways to begin working on self esteem. Great ones can be found anywhere, but 50 affirmations that specifically enhance self concept are provided in the back of this book. Making affirming statements a regular part of each day can help us feel more positive and more valuable!

To do:
- Choose three to five affirmations to begin using as daily mantras. You can choose the statements that reflect beliefs you already have about yourself and want to strengthen, or you can choose statements that reflect beliefs you don't *currently* have but would like to.

- You can dedicate specific time each day to focus and reflect on them. You can also help them seep into your subconscious by placing copies of your affirmations in conspicuous spots like your bathroom mirror, the fridge, your car dashboard, and your computer. The key is to make these positive and empowering thoughts a part of your core belief system.

Why it works:
Focusing on affirming statements helps us to introduce and strengthen positive beliefs in ourselves with repetition and reflection.

Self Esteem Activity #2
Fake It Til You Make It

Sometimes we just have to act *as if* we feel a certain way to get us through a particular experience. For many women, feeling confident is a challenge. But when we act as if we're confident, the ripple effects can be surprising.

To do:
- Pretend to be confident. Think of people you know with a lot of confidence and self awareness and act how you think they'd act.

- This works especially well if you've had time to figure out what confidence looks like to you so that you'll know what to do. For some people, confidence includes standing up straight, holding their head high, making eye contact, and having a firm handshake. What does it look like for you?

Why it works:
Our behaviors quickly begin to match our pretend confidence, which in turn increases our actual confidence. And others respond well to a self-assured person. This is the beginning of a positive and effective cycle that can be built on!

Self Esteem Activity #3
Past Achievements

Feeling successful is essential to good self esteem. In fact, it's impossible to feel good about ourselves if we feel like we never accomplish anything! Spending some time thinking about and appreciating our success is an often overlooked yet very powerful way to give our self esteem a big boost.

To do:
- Reflect on at least five things that you've accomplished in your life: anything that you're proud of like giving birth naturally, surviving cancer, traveling overseas, or getting your motorcycle license. If you're having a hard time coming up with accomplishments, view your life through the eyes of someone else for a more encouraging perspective.

- Reflect on these questions:
  1. Why was this achievement important to me?
  2. What does it say about me and my strengths?
  3. How can I apply what I learned from this successful experience to help me in the future?

Why it works:
Recognizing and appreciating our achievements shows us that we are capable and accomplished human beings...and reminds us that we will enjoy success again!

Self Esteem Activity #4
Give Yourself Permission

We often notice that when we are given permission to do something it seems much easier to do. It makes us feel like we're going with the grain and are doing the right thing. So we should go ahead and give ourselves permission to like ourselves. It's OK!

To do:

- Give yourself permission to be a flawed individual, an imperfect human.

- Choose to acknowledge both your weaknesses and your strengths and appreciate their role in making you who you are.

- Decide to like you for who and what you are: a work in progress!

Why it works:
Giving ourselves approval to like who we are now and who we are becoming is like taking the blinders off to reveal a whole new field of vision. We're free to look around and be OK with what we see!

Forgive Your Childhood

Nobody had a perfect childhood. Our parents probably did the best they could with the capabilities they had. And even if they didn't, there's no way to change that now. We should view our childhoods as a memory that provides valuable but non-defining information. We choose to take what we can from it, and then move on. As adults, we now have the opportunity and responsibility to shape our own future.

To do:
- Reflect on things in your childhood that negatively impacted you and understand the role they played in shaping who you are.

- Ask yourself these questions:
    1. Can I change my beliefs about myself, even if they've been with me since childhood?
    2. Am I willing to put to rest some of the hurtful memories from childhood that continue to impact me?
    3. How does it benefit me to hang on to old hurts?
    4. Do I deserve to feel better about myself today?

Why it works:
A lot of us attribute our low self esteem to issues stemming from our childhood so it's important to come to terms with what happened to us and figure out how to move on. We'll feel more relaxed, at peace, and capable when we do.

Self Esteem Activity #6
You've Got Talent!

While we may not all harbor some amazing secret genius, we do each have some things that we're good at...and those talents matter. We often think of "talents" as special abilities that are unique or amazing. But they can also refer to rather ordinary skills that you happen to be good at. Because none of us is great at everything, it's important to acknowledge the things we do well.

To do:
- Figure out what you're good at! Whether it's homemaking, creating, listening, helping, or building...they, and you, matter.

- Give yourself credit for your strengths by naming them–"I am good at keeping my paperwork neat and organized." "I make other people feel good by giving generous and sincere compliments."

- Appreciate how these talents benefit you— "Keeping my paperwork organized helps me feel prepared and in control over an important part of my life."

Why it works:
Our confidence gets a big boost by taking pride in what we do well!

Self Esteem Activity #7
Tune In to Your Values

Values are the rules that guide our lives and the ways in which we live them. We all have values but many of us haven't spent a lot of time identifying them or figuring out why they're important to us. Because our values shape our choices, becoming much more familiar with what they are and whether or not we're living up to them is important.

A very brief list of values includes courage, integrity, creativity, generosity, adventure, beauty, and honesty.

To do:
- Identify your ten most important values. There are a variety of books and online resources to help you name and clarify your values.

- Figure out which of your values are being left unfulfilled. If you value being compassionate, for example, but find yourself judging others a lot, you're not in sync with that value and have probably noticed a sense of conflict or discontent stemming from that.

- Make necessary changes to be true to who you are and who you want to be. This might mean that you're more deliberately thinking and acting in ways that get you closer to living by your values. Or this might mean that you have to re-assess whether a particular value is actually that important to you.

Why it works:
We feel a sense of peace and clarity within ourselves when we're living in harmony with our important values. And that's always a self esteem enhancer.

16

Self Esteem Activity #8
Forgive Yourself

Most of us have done things in the past that we're ashamed of or regret. Now it's time to let those feelings go. We've probably suffered enough from the actual consequences of these mistakes and hanging on to the bad feelings doesn't help us move our lives forward.

To do:
- Detail your indiscretion on paper, then burn it as a symbolic way of letting that regret go.

- Understand the person you were at the time—more naïve, less mature maybe—and love that you anyway.

- Give yourself a break by putting your mistake into perspective. One way to do this is to look at the mistake through the eyes of someone else and see if its significance diminishes. You can also pretend that a friend made the mistake—how would you respond to that friend?

Why it works:
Our self esteem can take a battering when we hang on to old mistakes. Regret and shame are two of the heaviest and most damaging emotions we can carry around so it's important to decide not to let them define us and to instead choose to move on.

Self Esteem Activity #9
Accept Compliments

This is a real challenge for a lot of women because we often feel like accepting a compliment means that we agree with the compliment—and heaven forbid we actually think something nice about ourselves! Learning how to graciously accept a compliment not only helps us to be polite and appreciative, it also shows other people how we expect to be treated, which is an amazing way to boost our self esteem!

To do:
- Train yourself to always smile and say "thank you" when complimented. Resist the desire to dispute or denigrate the compliment.

- Practice letting the kind words seep into your being instead of trying to shut them out. This may be hard to do in the moment, but make sure to take some time to review the compliment at a later time when you can allow yourself to feel the pride and positivity that come from praise.

- Make sure to sincerely compliment others too—you'll learn a lot about how their reaction to the compliment makes you as the giver feel. When you compliment someone and they deny, ignore, or denigrate your praise, it can make you feel ignored, letdown, and unheard. Knowing this might be the incentive you need to learn to accept compliments!

Why it works:
Graciously accepting compliments gives us the opportunity to really listen to and absorb positive feedback, practice accepting it instead of denying it, and make the giver feel good. This is a simple yet effective way to give our self esteem a lift.

Name Your Strengths

When our self esteem is low we tend to overlook and/or entirely forget the great qualities we do in fact possess. But each of us, no matter how much we beat up on ourselves, has positive characteristics that deserve to be recognized and validated. Appreciating our strengths doesn't make us boastful or self-centered; instead it makes us appreciate ourselves and our abilities.

To do:
- List at least five strengths you possess. These may be about your personality, your character, your education, or your skills.

- If you're having a hard time coming up with some strengths, ask yourself these questions:
  1. What do other people like about me?
  2. What is one thing I'm really good at?
  3. What's helped me get through tough times in the past?
  4. What's something I'm better at than are a lot of people?
  5. What am I most proud of about myself?

- Jot down what makes these particular strengths important, useful, and/or powerful. Reflect on their purpose and benefit to you.

Why it works:
Recognizing and appreciating our strengths lifts our spirit and sense of self. It also helps us focus on important personal qualities that may get overlooked. This is a great exercise to do at any time because recognizing our strengths is a great confidence, mood, and energy booster!

Self Esteem Activity #11
Do What You Love

We're in our comfort zone and feel most content when we're doing things we really love to do. So figuring out what those things are and finding the time to do them is an important ingredient for high self esteem. This exercise is great for women who are interested in creating some fulfilling hobbies.

To do:
- Decide what you really like to do: engaging in physical activities, participating in lively conversations, researching issues, meditating, being creative, taking long drives, organizing.

- Figure out how to do your favorite things more frequently.

- What is it about your favorite activities that make you feel good?

Why it works:
We naturally feel better about ourselves when we do things we love. Usually we feel fairly competent and comfortable with favorite activities so our confidence is boosted too.

Say It to Yourself

Sometimes we treat our friends better than we treat ourselves. For example, when a friend has a problem or is feeling down, we may expend more energy, kindness, and softness on her than we do on ourselves in similar situations. And while this compassion for others is noble, it's important to extend those same benefits to ourselves too, especially during troubling times.

To do:
- Imagine your closest friend curled up on the bed facing away from you. She's feeling bad about herself and you're trying to make her feel better.
  1. Write down at least 5 things you would say to, or do for, your friend.
  2. Now imagine your friend slowly turning towards you...and you see that who you thought was your friend in the bed is actually *you*.

- How does the actual act of saying kind things to yourself feel as opposed to saying kind things to a friend?

- How does it feel to *receive* this kind of support from yourself?

Why it works:
Treating ourselves well is a cornerstone of good self esteem. When we treat ourselves with generosity, kindness, and consideration, we are recognizing our value as human beings. This exercise is a good reminder to treat ourselves as we would treat a good friend, because we deserve it too.

Self Esteem Activity #13
Talk Nicely

We all have an internal monologue that influences our attitude and self concept. For a lot of us, negative self talk is a frequent and hurtful companion that hampers our ability to feel good about ourselves and our abilities. Positive self talk is the process of choosing encouraging rather than defeating internal commentary and is an amazingly effective way to improve your self esteem.

To do:

- Pay attention to your internal discussion, especially when you're feeling stressed, frustrated, anxious, or negative.

- When you notice negative self talk, stop your train of thought and either replace the negative talk with positive talk or redirect your thoughts completely. For example, change "I can't do this." To "I'm learning how to do this and I'll get better at it."

- Practice thinking nice things about yourself throughout the day like "I'm getting this project done faster than I thought I would," "My hair is looking pretty good today," and "I'm happy with how patient I was with my children."

Why it works:
Our thoughts determine our attitudes and behaviors. If we improve our ability to moderate our thoughts, then we take a giant step towards changing our actions and improving our attitudes.

Self Esteem Activity #14
Remember a Time...

We can use our past experiences to create more positive feelings for ourselves in the present. If we look at our past as a collection of learning experiences, then we're more likely to take those lessons and apply them to today. Our self esteem can be boosted especially by remembering a time when things were going well and we felt really good about ourselves.

To do:
- Think about a time when you felt good about yourself and ask these questions:
  1. What was going on in my life?
  2. What people did I choose to be with?
  3. What made that time so much different from now?
  4. What can I do to get back to feeling that way?

- Reflect on your control over your feelings and your ability to make your life what you'd like it to be.

Why it works:
Focusing on better times reminds us that not only is it possible to feel better again, but that we actually have the tools within ourselves to make it happen.

Self Esteem Activity #15
Do Your Body Good

Poor body image accounts for a lot of low self esteem issues—how we feel about our bodies directly relates to how we feel about ourselves in general. Working towards a healthier and more realistic body image is time well spent!

To do:
- Make a list of the top 10 things you like about your body or appearance.

- If this is hard to do, try thinking about your appearance from a different perspective and see what you come up with. For example, you may like your bellybutton, the way jeans fit your body, your earlobes, your shoulder muscles, that your "mustache" is easy to hide, or that it's not hard to find shoes that fit.

Why it works:
When we look at our bodies with more forgiving eyes, we'll be surprised at how much we actually like about our appearance. Making an effort to focus on the positive gives us a chance to appreciate the body we have and avoid getting derailed by harsh, undeserved, and debilitating self criticism.

Self Esteem Activity #16
Set Boundaries

Personal boundaries are the limits we set for our physical, emotional, and social space. Establishing personal boundaries is one of the best ways to avoid co-dependency and emotional burn out because they help us to stay true to ourselves and set and keep healthy limits.

To do:
- Be familiar with some signs of unhealthy boundaries including not being able to say "no," falling apart so someone else can take care of you, going against your personal values to please someone else, being too intimate too soon, and allowing your feelings to be determined by the feelings of another.

- Think about people or situations in which your boundaries may be tested or weakened; when you're feeling stressed, when you're around a domineering personality, when you're feeling insecure and lonely.

- In what ways can you prepare yourself to maintain your boundaries during challenging situations or with difficult people? Some options include knowing your limits so you can avoid or remove yourself from situations before your boundaries are breached, practice politely and firmly saying "no," knowing your values so you can tell when they're being neglected, practicing self control in sharing your physical and emotional self.

Why it works:
Having clear boundaries helps us feel really good about ourselves by strengthening our assertiveness and enhancing our self confidence.

Self Esteem Activity #17
Apologize

When we make a mistake, hurt someone's feelings, or do the wrong thing, it's important to acknowledge our regret. Admitting our mistakes and making amends can lift a big burden off our shoulders. When we apologize we admit our error and do our best to make up for it.

To do:
- Sincerely apologize to whoever needs to hear it.

- Decide on a verbal or written apology.

- Make sure to be humble and sincere and try not to give excuses.

- Ensure that you come to a place of personal peace and resolution after the apology no matter the reception it has received.

Why it works:
Apologizing develops our maturity and humility. Going through this process gives us a better sense of ourselves and our desire and ability to do the right thing.

Improving Your Connections

If only you could sense how important you are to the lives of those you meet; how important you can be to people you may never even dream of. There is something of yourself that you leave at every meeting with another person.
~ Fred Rogers

This section focuses on strengthening your sense of connectedness with individuals, your local community, and the world. Feeling united to people and things outside yourself is another key component to good self esteem.

A sense of belonging, feeling needed, and being connected with others helps us to stay grounded in reality, feel supported and loved, and feel a part of the bigger picture.

The activities in this section work directly on feelings of isolation, loneliness, and feeling stuck in your own head.

Self Esteem Activity #18
Do for Others

One surefire way to feel better about ourselves is to help someone else. It can be a very simple gesture or a grand offering, but the simple fact is that our feelings about ourselves are significantly boosted by doing something kind for another person.

To do:
- For "in person" gratification, focus your energies on those closest to you by taking cookies to a neighbor, treating your parents to supper, or having a special "date" with your child.

- To feel connected to a bigger mission, participate in a charity event or assemble care packages for troops.

Why it works:
Being generous allows us to step outside our own needs and concerns and directly uplift another person's sense of well being. Giving to others is a guaranteed way to feel better about ourselves!

Self Esteem Activity #19
Question Your Friends

Sometimes we need a little feedback and support from those closest to us to help give our self esteem a boost. Asking for this kind of feedback isn't for everyone, but for those brave enough to do it, the emotional benefits can be tremendous.

To do:
- Send the following questions to your friends and loved ones and ask for their feedback. Or come up with your own questions!
  1. What are some of the qualities about me you like best?
  2. What are three words that describe me?
  3. What's a good memory you have of me?
  4. What's something about me you really admire?
  5. If you knew I was feeling bad about myself, what would you say to me?

- Be careful that you choose people who will be kind, thoughtful, and positive in their responses. It won't do you any good to give these questions to your hyper critical aunt to complete.

Why it works:
Sometimes we need validation from others, especially when we're dealing with low self esteem issues. It's OK to ask for it, and loved ones are happy to help us feel better!

Self Esteem Activity #20
Feedback for Friends

For most women, maintaining good relationships is important. That's why when a friend is feeling down, we're quick to her aid. This exercise is a great way to give our friends an emotional boost while making us feel good too.

To do:
- Complete the following statements about a good friend and give them to her. Or make up your own statements!
  1. I think three of your best qualities are ...
  2. You are so good at _____ and I really admire that.
  3. One of the great things about you that you might sometimes forget is ...
  4. One of my favorite memories of you is ...
  5. Whenever you're feeling bad about yourself, I want you to remember that ...

Why it works:
This exercise reminds us why we've chosen special people to be in our lives and what value their friendship provides. It also encourages us to be generous with our positivity which comes back to us in multiples!

Bring Reality to Role Models

Many of us look up to and admire famous people from the past or present. Whether we admire heroes, leaders, or entertainers, it's easy to believe a famous person we admire is perfect or has a fortunate life when the reality is that even folks who reach the height of fame and success have weaknesses they struggle with too. Having role models is important but understanding their human frailties is essential for a fair and realistic perspective.

To do:
- Read quotes by and watch interviews of your role model.

- Read his/her biography and/or autobiography.

- Really pay attention to what you didn't already know—this person's tragedies, self image concerns, worries, views on social and world issues, childhood experiences.

- How does having a more complete understanding of this person affect your view of him/her? How does it affect your view of yourself and your own capabilities?

Why it works:
When you can look at a famous figure in a more realistic and complete way, you're closer to looking at yourself more realistically too.

33

Feel Patriotic

People who are proud to be a member of their country (native or adopted) feel a connection to past generations who worked hard to make their country what it is today.

To do:

- Read your country's founding documents and history.

- Find elements of your citizenship that make you proud, knowing that you don't have to agree with every aspect of your nation's history.

- Reflect on what you have because of where you live.

- Appreciate your opportunities.

- Think about what you have in common with your countrymen and women.

Why it works:
Understanding our country's journey from founding to today can be an empowering process. Feeling a connection with fellow citizens and those who've sacrificed gives us a greater sense of pride and belonging.

Self Esteem Activity #23
Connect to Your Ancestry

Connecting with the experiences of those who came before us and made our lives possible is an excellent way to feel proud of and attached to our family's past.

To do:
- Research your genealogy and learn who paved the way for your existence. This can be your biological family's history or the history of the family that's raised you.

- Listen to stories from your elders. Let your family history come alive through their stories and memories of generations gone by.

- Learn more about the parts of the country or world your ancestors came from and feel a deeper connection with those roots.

Why it works:
When we connect with our ancestry (biological or not), we strengthen the bonds with our family's history and strength. This sense of belonging and feeling deeply rooted connects us to the resilient people who paved the way. It can restore our sense of purpose and bonding to our family tree.

Self Esteem Activity #24
Meet New People

Making new friends, or at least interacting with different people, gives us a chance to get out of our heads and make some interpersonal connections. While it can feel nerve-wracking to converse with people for the first time, finding those people doesn't have to be hard at all!

To do:
- An easy way to meet new people and feel at least some level of comfort doing it is to look for events that center around your interests.

- While you can still look to your local newspaper or community park district for activities, also try www.meetup.com and www.craigslist.org to find local groups and events centered around a wide range of hobbies and interests.

- A good way to break the ice when you're meeting people for the first time is to ask how long they've been interested in the particular hobby, to tell them this is your first time at the event, or to compliment something about the person.

Why it works:
Meeting new people helps us hone our conversational and social skills and allows us to practice presenting our best selves.

Self Esteem Activity #25
Your Civic Duty

Getting involved in civic opportunities on a community or national level is an option available to all of us. As citizens of our nation, we have a lot to offer for its continued success and we may be surprised at the attitude boost we get from becoming more involved in our local and national communities.

To do:
- Keep in touch with your elected local and national representatives.

- Make your voice heard on issues that matter to you, even in non-election years.

- Volunteer in the schools by offering tutoring, coaching, or computer training.

- Help to beautify your community by picking up trash along the roads or volunteering to plant flowers in public parks.

Why it works:
Doing for our community and country gives us a sense of connection and belonging that keeps us feeling grounded, useful, and needed.

Self Esteem Activity # 26
Strengthen Relationships

Relationships are important for everyone, but as women, maintaining good relationships is *essential* to our sense of community and level of satisfaction.

To do:

- Revive a relationship by sending a greeting card to an old friend.

- Leave a voicemail for someone you want to connect with again.

- Take the time to write a long email to a family member who misses you.

- Set reminders on your calendar to regularly reach out to people important to you—remember that it doesn't have to be a big gesture.

Why it works:
Connecting with others reduces our sense of isolation and strengthens important bonds. Doing something that makes others feel good boosts our sense of generosity and makes us feel good too!

<u>Controlling Your Destiny</u>

If you don't run your own life, somebody else will.
~ John Atkinson

This section focuses on strengthening your sense of power and control over the direction of your life. Feeling like the boss of your own personal path is a key component to good self esteem.

When you feel victimized and out of control it's hard to feel in charge of your life's direction. And when you're not in control of where you're going, it's hard to feel good about yourself.

The activities in this section work directly on enhancing your ability to make choices that are in your best interests and help you feel strong and sure-footed, even during uncertain times.

Self Esteem Activity #27
Be Inspired

It's an incredible fact that every month more than a million people will search online for inspiration. We all instinctively know that it's a lot harder to get where we want to go (or do what we need to do) if we don't feel inspired or motivated.

To do:
- Find *inspirational quotes* that speak to you. Even a one or two line statement can evoke a lot of emotion and energy.

- Listen to *inspiring music* while multi-tasking or enjoying a quiet moment. You may have particular songs in mind that inspire you or you could listen to music that is made to be inspirational.

- Read an *inspiring story*. Reading about how someone overcame tragedies, performed amazing feats, or maintained optimism through challenges can move and encourage you in your own life.

- Whether you choose inspirational quotes, music, or stories, make sure you spend some time reflecting on the message you take from the activity and ask yourself:
  1. Why do I connect with this?
  2. How does this apply to me?
  3. How can I use this to help me move forward?

Why it works:
Inspirational quotes, music, and stories can excite us to do what we want to do and be who we want to be. We can use the motivation, appreciation, and encouragement we feel to move our lives forward with a purpose!

Self Esteem Activity #28
Sacrifice

When we choose to give up something important to us (time, money, possessions) for the benefit of someone else, we feel a surge of happiness and generosity. Making the choice to give what we have allows us to actively put the needs of others ahead of our own status quo. And deciding to sacrifice for others is a purposeful way to defeat the common misunderstanding that we need more in order to feel better about ourselves.

To do:
- Spend a Saturday at the pound helping with animal care.

- Donate money to a charity you believe in.

- Instead of a garage sale this year, give your items to Goodwill or another charitable organization.

- Choose to give anonymously by having bouquets of flowers delivered to local nursing home residents or leaving an envelope of cash at a needy friend's door.

Why it works:
Sacrificing allows you to focus on and appreciate your own good fortune and view your success through a different lens. It's a great way to take charge of your self esteem.

Self Esteem Activity #29
Be Brave

To grow as individuals, we need to step out of our comfort zones and push through worrisome feelings. It's important to try new and scary things that we wouldn't typically do. This is a great way to explore other parts of our personality that may not get much attention. This type of challenge is rarely easy, but the benefits to our self esteem can be amazing!

To do:
- Take a new route to work, talk to strangers, enroll in a class, or volunteer to give a presentation at a work event.

- If you tend to be introverted and shy, do something that challenges that part of you like taking a dance class, meeting your neighbors, or running for an office in the PTO.

- After your "challenge," think about how it made you feel. Even if the activity itself didn't feel successful, you deserve to be proud for being brave and determined.

Why it works:
A sense of success, especially when trying something different and/or difficult, increases our confidence, determination, and satisfaction. If these are unfamiliar feelings, then this is a great opportunity to safely develop them!

A New You

Changing the look of a room can give it a whole new feeling...and that goes for us too! Sometimes refreshing our physical appearance can change our entire perspective on ourselves and lift our attitude. A new look can give us a sense of lightness, new beginnings, and confidence that ripples throughout our entire being.

To do:

- Find a picture of a hair style you like or ask your stylist what she thinks will work best for your face and lifestyle. Then be brave and go for it!

- Schedule an appointment at a department store makeup counter for a free makeover. Pay attention to how the makeup is applied so you can replicate the new look at home.

- Even if this exercise sounds silly or unlike you, don't discount the impact a new look can have on your sense of self. The attention and pampering that are inherent in visits with stylists are added benefits!

Why it works:
A fresh look and feel can jump start a whole new attitude. Getting professional attention on our appearance can do wonders for our self image and confidence!

Self Esteem Activity # 31
Quiet Down

Daily life for a lot of us has gotten incredibly busy and chaotic. With the convenience of cell phones and the internet comes the burden of always being available and rarely having uninterrupted, sacred time. We all need quiet time to rejuvenate our spirits, to reconnect with ourselves, and to decompress from the demands of life. When our days are demanding and hectic, quiet reflective time is an important part of becoming and staying balanced and feeling at peace with ourselves.

To do:
- Spend some time meditating or journaling to help you connect with your own spirit and sense of contentment.

- Set aside time each day to just focus on how your body is feeling and practice some relaxation techniques.

- Use quiet time to daydream about your goals and allow the peace that comes with being still and calm re-energize your ambitions.

Why it works:
Connecting with our inner selves is one way to feel more peaceful and appreciative of who and what we are—as human beings, as women, and as ourselves.

Self Esteem Activity #32
Good News Only

It's nearly impossible to have high self esteem if you have a negative world view. That's because we are products and citizens of the world and cannot like ourselves too much if we dislike our environment. That's why it's so important to be proactive in seeking out positivity and optimism to help re-establish a more realistic world view. While it can be hard to focus on, let alone find, positive news in our calamity-driven media—it is possible!

To do:
- Search online for good news and you'll come up with a variety of sources to help remind you of the beautiful, generous, and amazing world we live in.

- Figure out how to reduce the negative information you're bombarded with each day, such as consuming less of the mainstream media or avoiding negative people.

Why it works:
Reading about positive news and avoiding the negative can help us to raise our spirits, focus on optimism, and feel connected to a more hopeful and caring world.

Self Esteem Activity #33
Be Open to Change

We are often resistant to change because it can feel scary, difficult, and uncertain. But being open to change ensures that we don't miss an opportunity to make good adjustments in our lives. It also allows us to see our options and appreciate our choices. At the very least, being open to change means we're more likely to have new and exciting experiences!

To do:

- Shake things up. Try out a new recipe for a familiar dish. Choose a new attitude towards an old problem. Try a new type of exercise program. Be aware of and open to your choices—from big to small!

- Take note of how doing something different makes you feel. Do you notice your horizon seems to feel a little wider?

- Recognize that being open to change opens up choices for you and revel in the opportunity to decide on the best option.

Why it works:
Being open to change does two things. First, we're reminded that we're always capable of growth and never have to settle for being stagnant. Second, we give ourselves the opportunity to make informed decisions based on the options we've tried. Choosing an option based on information gives us more freedom and confidence than choosing an option because we feel limited.

Self Esteem Activity #34
Get Out of Your Way

Many of us are responsible for sabotaging our own progress and success. At times, we are all guilty of using self sabotage techniques when we're feeling overwhelmed, apprehensive, or insecure. While self sabotage is very common, it can become a problem when it prevents us from progressing and reaching the success we deserve. Some self sabotage techniques are procrastinating, being inflexible, being indecisiveness, withdrawing, having unrealistic expectations, and fearing failure.

To do:
- Ask yourself these questions:
  1. What self-sabotage methods hold me back most often?
  2. When are they most likely to happen? For example, when my spouse hurts my feelings, when I'm overwhelmed by my job responsibilities, when I'm apprehensive about a potential conflict.
  3. What can I do to diminish them? While it's impossible to completely eliminate the use of self sabotage, it is entirely possible to reduce their effects by planning ahead for difficult situations, reinforcing your sense of self before dealing with difficult people, and being aware of your typical patterns.

Why it works:
Becoming more aware of our favorite self sabotage techniques gives us a real head start towards figuring out the appropriate way to diminish their effects. Once we get out of our own way and become an asset rather than a roadblock to accomplishing our goals, our self esteem will soar!

Set SMART Goals

It's easy to be hard on ourselves and feel unsuccessful when we never seem to achieve our goals. In fact, the first few months in a new year can be some of the most frustrating for those of us who set New Year's Resolutions because that's when it becomes apparent that we're not going to reach those goals this year either. One of the biggest reasons that we don't accomplish what we set out to do is that most of the time we don't set the right kind of goals. Take the time and effort to set SMART goals so your destination is clear and doable.

To do:
- Set a goal that is:
    Specific—detailed and precise, clear and concise
    Measurable—how will you know when you've reached your goal?
    Attainable—it is physically and emotionally possible for you to reach this goal
    Realistic—there's a good chance that you'll do what you need to do to achieve this goal
    Timely—set a time frame for achieving this goal

- Be open to tweaking this goal as time goes on. One of the biggest indicators of future success is your flexibility in making necessary adjustments when circumstances change.

Why it works:
Feeling successful is important. When we're struggling with low self esteem, it is *essential*. Setting SMART goals ensures that we start with a realistic and attainable plan of action.

Self Esteem Activity #36
Slow Down

It's impossible to be able to appreciate all we have and all we are when we always live life at a breakneck pace. When we take the time to slow down, we have more time and focus to reflect on the big issues that are meaningful to our happiness.

To do:
- For a quick vacation from the chaos of life, mentally rejuvenate at the library by browsing through the stacks, reading in a quiet corner, and soaking in the ambience.

- Enjoy and appreciate your sustenance by eating more slowly.

- When you're in a long line at the grocery store, turn a necessary chore into a chance to relax by taking advantage of the time to yourself: people watch, browse through the checkout magazines, or just take a mental time out and let yourself daydream.

Why it works:
When we take the time to slow things down, we notice the unique and wonderful nuances that make up our environment. When we give ourselves time to slow down, we're able to soak in the small joys life gives us every day.

Self Esteem Activity #37
What Not to Wear

Most of us feel more comfortable in certain clothes. If this sounds familiar to you, then you know the role your clothes play in your self-image. When you're feeling good about yourself, you're more likely to feel comfortable in a variety of clothes and accessories. But when you're stuck in a funk and feeling bad about yourself, one of the first things that fly out the window is your desire to maintain your appearance. It's easy then to fall into a negative cycle that can be really damaging to your self-image. If how you look plays a big role in how you feel about yourself, then this topic is well worth some extra attention!

To do:
- Do you have a girlfriend whose personal style you admire? Invite her over for a clothing makeover by getting her advice on your outfits, shoes, and accessories. She'll be able to help you decide what looks best on your body and what looks are current and trendy.

- Take her shopping with you to find some new clothes that look great and make you feel great too.

- Truly listen to the positive feedback you get; kind words from someone you admire and look up to mean a lot.

Why it works:
If we feel comfortable in our clothes and like how they make us look, we'll reflect it in our confidence and self esteem.

Self Esteem Activity #38
Plant a Seed

Often we expect big personal changes to occur immediately. And when things don't work that way, we can get discouraged and lose our motivation. It's important to keep our expectations realistic, appreciate the value of "slow and steady," and understand our responsibility for our own development and sense of self. One tangible way to absorb these lessons is to play an integral role in growing a plant from seed.

To do:
- Get the information and help you need to plant a seed, nurture it, and watch it grow.

- Pay attention to how you play your role—involved or detached, interested or distracted, caring or brusque. How does it feel to watch the daily changes in your plant?

- What lessons can you take from this experience and apply to your own development journey?

- What has this exercise taught you about yourself?

- If your plant didn't grow, what different action could you have taken to change the outcome?

Why it works:
Being responsible for something else's growth and success gives us a sense of pride and accomplishment. Applying the lessons we learn to our own lives can provide a fresh perspective on our own growth and sense of success.

Take Care of Yourself

We all have choices over what foods we eat, whether or not we use our bodies, how we spend our time, and what attitude we have. When we treat our body and mind well, we automatically feel better about ourselves and our ability to make good decisions. Being conscientious about the choices we make and whether or not they're helping us become who you want to be is a powerful way to take control of our self esteem.

To do:
- Associate with people who support and love you.

- Reduce your junk food and increase your veggie, fruit, and whole grain consumption.

- Spend less time in front of the TV or computer.

- Reduce your stress by actively practicing relaxation techniques and avoiding tense environments.

- Get your body moving and stretching.

- Actively seek out positive people, thoughts, and situations while reducing your exposure to the negative.

Why it works:
When we realize that we have the power to decide how we're going to live and feel, we understand that we're in control, confident, and capable.

Self Esteem Activity #40
Picture It

Using our own creativity to improve our environment is an amazingly powerful way to feel better about our space and our ability to improve it. One simple yet effective way to engage our imagination, beautify our surroundings, and feel proud of our abilities is to take photographs that reflect our interests and help us feel good about ourselves.

To do:
- Take pictures of a wide variety of scenes that make you feel good, inspired, hopeful, and energized.

- Enlarge and/or frame the photos that best represent the attitude you want your space to radiate.

- Decorate your environment with the fruits of your creative labor!

Why it works:
Using our own creativity to revamp our surroundings gives us a real sense of "can do" and pride. When we feel more positive about our environment we get an automatic motivation and mood boost!

Take Charge of Your Health

Many of us are afraid of evaluating the state of our physical health. We worry about getting bad news so we avoid keeping up with ordinary health procedures. But there is a definite sense of relief that can come from knowing what our health status is and knowing what issues we're dealing with. This knowledge gives us choices and a way to take control of our wellbeing. Being an active participant in our health care is an excellent way to feel better about ourselves.

To do:
- Get your teeth professionally cleaned.

- See a foot specialist if you have foot issues.

- Get your vision tested.

Why it works:
Taking care of our health is important, and seeking the professional services we need to function at our best is a great way to put our well being as a top priority. When we take care of ourselves, our sense of self worth is in a good place.

Self Esteem Activity #42
Keep a Diary

Recording our life experience, either as a private journal or a public blog, is a great way to document our life and share our knowledge. Putting our experiences and feelings down on paper can help validate their importance and their impact on our lives. It's also a great way to stay connected to and be remembered by future generations.

To do:
- Write about particular life experiences and your feelings about them.

- Journal about your dreams for the future.

- Write about your important relationships with other people.

- Share as much or as little as you feel comfortable with, keeping in mind that unless you destroy your writings, they will most likely be read by others at some point.

Why it works:
When we look back over our life's writings, we can appreciate all that we've experienced and accomplished. That gives us a greater perspective on where we've been and where we're headed!

Self Esteem Activity #43
Lighten Up

It's easier to feel good about ourselves when we seek out the lighter side of life. Because sometimes in even our darkest moments, a perfectly timed joke from a good friend can shine a ray of light through the fog of frustration. When we don't take ourselves, or life, too seriously, we're able to shake off mistakes and rebound from frustration much quicker. Plus, being able to find humor in ourselves and our frustrations makes us more pleasant to be around!

To do:
- Search for funny stories, jokes, videos, or TV shows that you enjoy.

- Remind yourself throughout the day to be more lighthearted and less serious.

- Practice lightening up before you respond to a frustrating situation or an annoying person.

- Get in touch with your sense of fun and your ability to laugh at yourself.

Why it works:
It makes sense that we feel better about ourselves and the world when we're smiling and having a good time. For many of us, that doesn't always come naturally so purposefully seeking out the lighter side of life is a great way to give ourselves an attitude boost.

Practice the "Wright" Way

Many people feel like handwriting is becoming less and less important in this technological era. While that may be true, the fact remains that penmanship is one of the natural ways we express our personal style and attitude. Our handwriting is unique to each of us, like a finger print, and can show how we think of ourselves and influence how others perceive us too. If our penmanship hasn't gotten much attention lately, it might be something interesting to focus on because improving it can be a great way to boost our self image.

To do:
- Practice your penmanship by writing more slowly and more deliberately; remember the pride you felt as a young student first learning to write your letters?

- Write cards to friends and family who will enjoy receiving a very personal message from you.

- Pay attention to the nuances of your written word to understand what makes your style unique to you.

- Speculate what a handwriting analyst would presume about you.

Why it works:
Our handwriting is a reflection on us and one way we can share ourselves with the world. Working to improve it means we care about how others perceive us and gives us a sense of pride as we create beautifully written words that mirror our unique styles.

Self Esteem Activity #45
Set the Mood

In order to feel and operate our best, we need to live and work in environments that fulfill our needs. So for those of us who are affected by the mood of our environment, let's take control over how it looks! With some planning and simple steps, we can make it reflect our interests, tastes, and fulfillment.

To do:
- Decorate with artificial flowers for natural-looking beauty all year long.

- Use your favorite colors for walls, accents, or special touches.

- Figure out what visuals (figurines, posters, quotations, personal creations, family pictures, affirmations) you enjoy for motivation, relaxation, confidence, energy, or empowerment and surround yourself with them.

Why it works:
We are our happiest and most productive when we feel comfortable and inspired in our environment.

Self Esteem Activity #46
Make a Good Meal

For those of us who don't consider ourselves good in the kitchen, this exercise may not sound appealing. But if you can read a recipe and successfully buy groceries, you'll be able to make a simple yet wonderful meal. And creating a meal for ourselves or our loved ones is a simple (and yummy) way to feel proud and accomplished.

To do:
- Find a recipe that looks good to you (search online, at your local library or bookstore, or ask a friend). There are a million recipe books with every type of theme you could imagine: using particular ingredients, following special dietary guidelines, cooking at a professional level, using 5 ingredients or fewer, cooking for one, and many more.

- If cooking is unfamiliar territory for you, use lots of patience and good humor!

- Even if it's a meal for one, serve your creation on dishes you like, at a table that looks nice, and in a room that is peaceful and comforting.

Why it works:
Creating enjoyable food from scratch all by ourselves is one of the purest and most primal ways to feel proud, resourceful, and surprisingly content.

Self Esteem Activity #47
Solve a Problem

Using our skills, knowledge, and determination to solve a problem is an immediate confidence, resourcefulness, and satisfaction booster. In fact, when we begin to successfully resolve issues, we begin to build up our sense of achievement and the belief that we can overcome any challenge. And that's a great way to increase our self esteem!

To do:

- Call your phone company to dispute a questionable charge, learn to fix your leaky bathroom faucet, or put together a bookshelf.

- Use problem solving as an opportunity to learn something new or practice your negotiation skills.

- While relationships can present plenty of problems, for this exercise its best to choose a problem that is well defined and straightforward so that you have a high chance of finding and implementing a practical solution.

Why it works:
Finding solutions to problems that have a clear-cut and step-by-step solution gives us a chance to feel successful and good about ourselves while managing a challenge effectively.

Self Esteem Activity #48
Produce Endorphins

Producing endorphins is our body's natural solution to feeling low. We have the ability to do things that encourage our body to produce these chemicals so we can essentially activate them as needed.

To do:
- Try some form of exercise like walking briskly for 30 minutes.

- Enjoy dishes with spicy foods like hot peppers, horseradish or wasabi.

- Listen to inspiring music.

- Get an adrenalin rush by watching a scary movie, riding a roller coaster, or singing karaoke.

Why it works:
Endorphins are the body's way of lowering stress, reducing pain, and giving us more energy. They are naturally occurring chemicals that help us to feel better about ourselves and our challenges.

50 Positive Affirmations on
How to Love Yourself!

1. My inner voice guides me in every moment.

2. I am centered, calm and clear.

3. When I know where I'm going, getting there is a cinch!

4. Today I am completely tuned in to my inner wisdom.

5. I trust my feelings and insights.

6. I am filled with light, love and peace.

7. I treat myself with kindness and respect.

8. I don't have to be perfect; I just have to be me.

9. I give myself permission to shine.

10. I honor the best parts of myself and share them with others

11. I'm proud of all I have accomplished.

12. I love myself no matter what.

13. I am grateful for the people in my life.

14. I deserve to be loved and I allow myself to be loved.

15. Today I open my mind to the endless opportunities surrounding me.

16. All is well, right here, right now.

17. Peace begins with a conscious choice.

18. Today I embrace simplicity, peace and solace.

19. A peaceful heart makes for a peaceful life.

20. The better I know myself, the clearer my purpose becomes.

21. My unique skills and talents can make a profound difference in the world.

22. Today I follow my heart and discover my destiny.

23. I am meant to do great things.

24. I am limited only by my vision of what is possible.

25. Today I present my love, passion, talent and joy as a gift to the world.

26. I need not know the entire journey in order to take one step.

27. I fulfill my life purpose by starting here, right now.

28. My life purpose can be whatever I decide to make it.

29. Fear is only a feeling; it cannot hold me back.

30. I know that I can master anything if I do it enough times.

31. Today I am willing to fail in order to succeed.

32. I believe that I have the strength to make my dreams come true.

33. I'm going to relax and have fun with this, no matter what the outcome may be.

34. I'm proud of myself for even daring to try; many people won't even do that!

35. Today I put my full trust in my inner guidance.

36. I grow in strength with every forward step I take.

37. I release my hesitation and make room for victory!

38. With a solid plan and a belief in myself, there's nothing I can't do.

39. Today I love my body fully, deeply and joyfully.

40. My body has its own wisdom and I trust that wisdom completely.

41. My body is simply a projection of my beliefs about myself.

42. I am growing more beautiful and luminous day by day.

43. I choose to see the divine perfection in every cell of my body.

44. As I love myself, I allow others to love me too.

45. Flaws are transformed by love and acceptance.

46. Today I choose to honor my beauty, my strength and my uniqueness.

47. I love the way I feel when I take good care of myself.

48. Today my own well-being is my top priority.

49. My energy and vitality are increasing every day.

50. I am only in control of myself. What a relief!

About the Author

Corinna Bowers is a life coach who helps women to feel more confident, connected, and accomplished. She compiled this book in response to her clients' pleas for an effective and personal self esteem building resource that speaks directly to their dreams and challenges.

Corinna has spent most of her adult life in the helping profession, from being a therapist for abuse survivors to being a relationship coach for a popular online service. She earned a Master's degree in counseling from Northern Illinois University, but the vast majority of her "schooling" came from her own life experiences and her professional and personal interactions with others.

Corinna has walked with overwhelmed women through some of their most frustrating and challenging times and she's paid attention. She's asked questions. And she's learned a lot. She has become very familiar with many women's most common fears, challenges, and underestimated strengths. She knows what it takes to work through them to find ultimate success.

What clients say about coaching with Corinna:

> "You have helped me to pinpoint some of my biggest insecurity points that I habitually go back to and I am learning to set goals and priorities to help myself get past those - and I am better able to recognize when I am falling back into those insecurities."

> "Thanks again for your help! I am enjoying this more than I ever thought. And to think I was so nervous about doing this. This has been a very good thing for me. I actually feel more positive and in control with my life which is great!"

"I think Corinna helped me to find the person I once was and to be an even better person who is in tune to their feelings and the feelings of others. My life is a more positive adventure with much hope for the future. And I have the skills and knowledge to get myself back on track should I need it in the future."

Originally from the Chicago land area, Corinna now lives with her husband and their two young children in rural Tennessee.

She is a member of the Tennessee Coaches Alliance.

For more information on Corinna, her coaching services, and her other self help products, visit her website at www.focused-momentum-lifecoach.com.